W9-CFQ-413

Plastics

By Kate Bedford

Stargazer Books

© Aladdin Books Ltd 2006

Designed and produced by
Aladdin Books Ltd

First published in the
United States in 2006 by
Stargazer Books
c/o The Creative Company
123 South Broad Street
P.O. Box 227
Mankato, Minnesota 56002

Printed in Malaysia

Editor:
Harriet Brown

Designers:
Flick, Book Design and Graphics
Simon Morse

Picture Researchers:
Alexa Brown and Fiona Patchett

Illustrations:
Q2A Creative

Literacy consultant:
Jackie Holderness — former Senior
Lecturer in Primary Education,
Westminster Institute,
Oxford Brookes University

*Library of Congress Cataloging-in-
Publication Data*

Bedford, Kate.
    Plastics / by Kate Bedford.
        p. cm. -- (World about us)
    Includes index.
    ISBN 1-59604-042-4
    1. Plastics--Juvenile literature.
    I. Title. II. World about us
    (North Mankato, Minn.)

TP1125.B43 2005
620.1'923--dc22
                                    2005041813

CONTENTS

Notes to parents and teachers	4
What is plastic?	6
Plastic history	8
How is plastic made?	10
Different plastics	12
Making things with plastic	14
Bubbly plastic	16
All wrapped up	18
Plastic clothes	20
Plastics for health	22
The problem with plastic	24
Recycling plastic	26
Plastic for the future	28
See how much you know!	30
Key words	31
Glossary	31
Index	32

Notes to parents and teachers

This series has been developed for group use in the classroom, as well as for children reading alone. In particular, its text on two levels allows children of mixed abilities to enjoy reading about the same topic. The larger size text (A, below) offers apprentice readers a simplified text. This simplified text is used in the introduction to each chapter and in the picture captions. This font is part of the © Sassoon family of fonts whose maximum legibility is recommended for early readers. The smaller size text (B, below) offers a more challenging read for older or more able readers.

Bubbly plastic

Plastic can be made into a foam. Foam is made by blowing bubbles of gas into melted plastic.

A

 Plastic foam helps to keep things warm.

Plastic foam is a good heat insulator. This means it does not let heat pass through it.

B

Questions, key words, and glossary

Each spread ends with a question that parents and teachers can use to discuss and develop further ideas and concepts. Further questions are provided in a quiz on page 30. A reduced version of pages 30 and 31 is shown below. The illustrated "Key words" section is provided as a revision tool, particularly for apprentice readers, in order to help with spelling, writing, and guided reading. The glossary is for more able or older readers.

In addition to the glossary's role as a reference aid, it is also designed to reinforce new vocabulary and provide a tool for further discussion and revision. When glossary terms first appear in the text they are highlighted in bold.

 See how much you know!

What is most plastic made from?

How are plastic gloves made?

Why is plastic used to make electric sockets and to cover wires?

Why are plastic bottles used for storing chemicals?

What happens to plastic things that are thrown away?

How can you tell what type of plastic a container is made from?

What will plastic be made from in the future?

What plastic items could you reuse?

Key words

Bottle

A

Fabric

Foam   **Material**

Oil rig   **Recycling**

Tube   **Wrapping**

Teeth

Glossary

Biodegradable—When a material can be decayed by bacteria and other tiny animals.
Durable—When something is hard-wearing and lasts for a long time.
Flexible—Something that can easily bend.
Incinerator—A fire where unwanted things are burned and turned to ashes.
Insulator—A material or substance that does not let heat pass through it easily.
Landfill site—A huge hole in the ground where garbage is burned.
Pollution—Harmful chemicals, gases or garbage that damage the environment.
Resistant—When a material is unharmed by things such as chemicals or heat.

B

What is plastic?

Plastic is a man-made material. It is an amazing material that is used to make many different things. Every day, all over the world, people use or wear things made from plastic.

◄ **Most plastic is made from oil.**

Crude oil is the raw material that most plastics are made from. Oil is a fossil fuel. It is made from the remains of tiny aquatic plants and animals that lived millions of years ago. Today, oil is found in rocks that are deep under the ground or under the sea.

All these things are made from plastic.

Plastic is a waterproof material. This means that it doesn't let water pass through it.

Unlike metal and wood, plastic does not rust or rot.

Electricity does not pass through plastic so it is used to make sockets and cover metal wires to keep us safe.

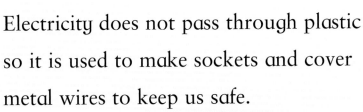

Plastic can be made in many different colors and formed into many different shapes.

 What plastic objects can you see around you?

Plastic history

Around 150 years ago, people did not have plastic things. Now plastic has become an important part of our everyday lives. Hundreds of different types of plastic have been invented. Think about how many plastic things you use each day.

◀ Cotton plants were used to make the first plastic.

The first plastic was made in 1862 from cellulose, which is a material found in plants. Alexander Parkes used cotton to make a plastic called celluloid that could be molded into many different shapes. This first plastic was used to make ornaments, cuffs, and collars.

◀ The telephone here is made from coal tar.

In 1907, a new plastic called Bakelite was made from coal tar. This plastic could be molded into any shape and it would not burn, boil, or melt once it had set hard. It was used to make telephones and radios.

Coal tar

Bakelite telephone

This surfboard is made from a new strong type of plastic.

New plastics have been invented that are strong, **durable**, light, and **flexible**. They are used to make sports equipment such as windsurf boards, ropes, and bullet-proof vests.

 What were toys made from before plastic was invented?

How is plastic made?

Oil is drilled and pumped out of rocks in the ground. Sometimes, oil is found in rocks under the sea. A platform called an oil rig is used to reach undersea oil. It stands or floats in the sea and drills the oil from the rocks.

◀ **Oil is taken here to be made into different things**.

Crude oil is taken to an oil refinery by a pipeline or huge oil tanker (ship). The refinery is like a huge factory where the oil will be separated into different things. Care must be taken when transporting oil. If the oil spills it can damage the natural environment.

The oil is heated and separated in a big tower.

The oil is separated into different chemicals by heating it in a huge tower. As the oil gets hotter the different chemicals in it boil, turn into gases, and separate out. When the separate gases cool down again, they turn back into liquids. The liquids are collected. Naptha is one of these liquids. Naptha is turned into a plastic called polythene, which is used to make many different plastics.

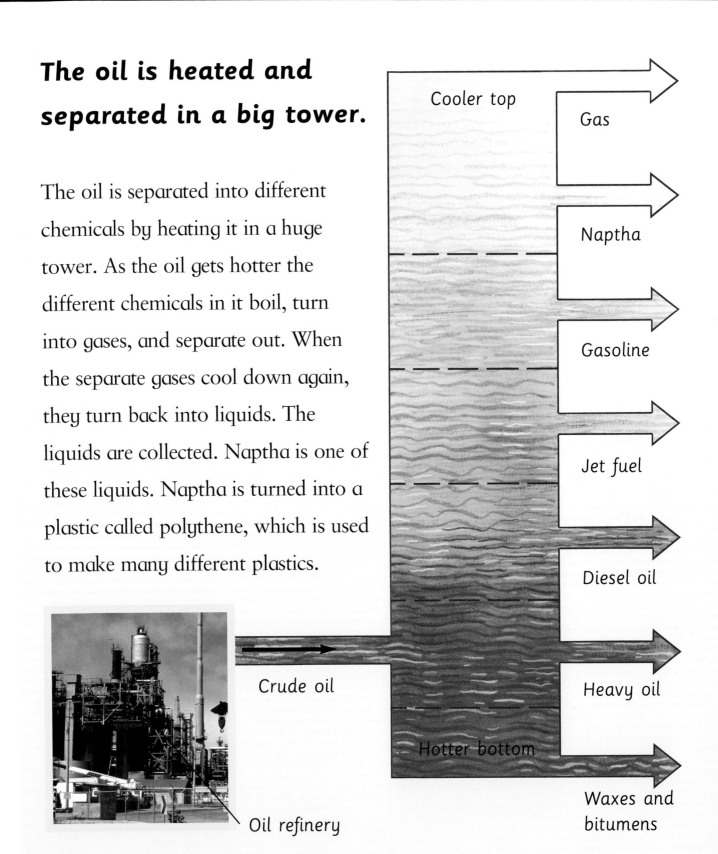

Cooler top

Gas

Naptha

Gasoline

Jet fuel

Diesel oil

Heavy oil

Hotter bottom

Waxes and bitumens

Crude oil

Oil refinery

 In what ways could oil damage the environment?

Different plastics

There are hundreds of different kinds of plastic. Some plastics are hard and others are soft and bendable. Plastic can be thin, thick, colored, or see-through. Plastic is a very useful material and we use it in many different ways.

Plastic bottles

Compact disc

◀ These things are made from different types of plastic.

There are two different groups of plastic. The plastics in one group melt when they are heated, and become solid again when they cool. This group of plastics are used to make bottles and clothing. The other group of plastics do not change shape when they are heated. They are used to make objects such as saucepan handles and CDs.

Many of the things we use are made from plastic.

► **Acrylic** is hard, strong, and transparent. It is used in clothing, reflectors, paints, signs, and safety "glass."

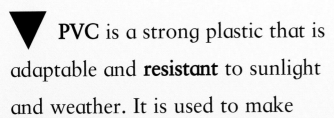

▲ **Polycarbonate** is a clear, strong plastic. It is used to make windows, household equipment, and road signs.

▼ **PVC** is a strong plastic that is adaptable and **resistant** to sunlight and weather. It is used to make window frames, clothes, and artificial leather.

▲ **Polystyrene** is light and brittle. It can be made into a foam that is used for packaging and lifejackets.

 What plastic items have you used today?

Making things with plastic

There are different ways of making plastic into the shapes we need. Many plastic objects are made using molds so they are all exactly the same. This means that plastic objects, such as Lego® building blocks, will fit together.

◀ **These bottles were shaped by a mold.**

Plastic bottles are made by a method called blow molding. A tube with a blob of runny plastic on the end is put inside a mold. Air is blown down the tube. The plastic inside the mold blows up like a balloon. It presses against the mold to make a hollow bottle shape.

Hand-shaped molds are dipped in plastic.

Plastic gloves are made by dip-molding. A solid hand-shaped mold is dipped into hot, liquid plastic. It comes out covered in a thin layer of plastic. When the plastic is set and dry, the finished glove is peeled off the mold.

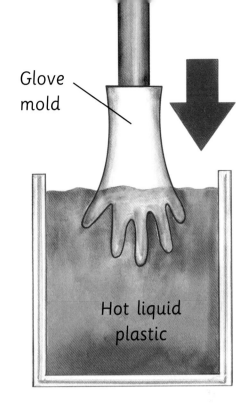

Glove mold

Hot liquid plastic

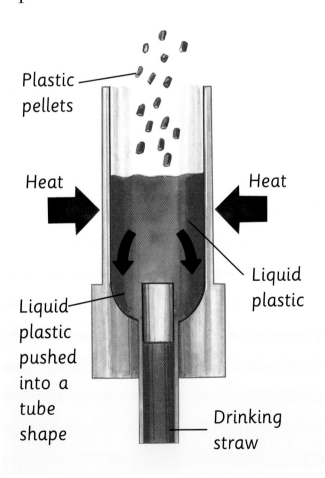

Plastic pellets

Heat

Heat

Liquid plastic

Liquid plastic pushed into a tube shape

Drinking straw

Plastic is squeezed through a hole to make a drinking straw.

Drinking straws are made by a method called extrusion. Hot, runny plastic is forced through a hole. As the plastic pushes out through the hole, it forms into a tube shape, just like icing piped onto a cake.

 How do you think plastic cups are made?

Bubbly plastic

Plastic can be made into a foam. Foam is made by blowing bubbles of gas into melted plastic. Some foams have very tiny bubbles inside, and others have bubbles that are big enough to see. Plastic foams are used in many different ways.

◀ **Plastic foam helps to keep things warm.**

Plastic foam is a good heat **insulator**. This means it does not let heat pass through it. We use plastic to insulate our homes and stop heat being lost through the walls and roof. Buildings can be insulated by putting sheets of foam behind walls, floors, or ceilings. We also use plastic foam to keep food and drinks warm.

◀ **Foam plastic is used to make furniture.**

The soft furniture that we use in our homes is filled with spongy plastic foam. The air bubbles in the foam make it soft to sit on. Some foam gives off dangerous fumes if it catches fire. New furniture is made with foam that doesn't easily burn.

Plastic foam helps to keep things safe from knocks.

Polystyrene plastic is used to package fragile objects that may easily get broken. The small pieces of polystyrene fit around an object and protect it against knocks. Polystyrene is strong but lightweight. It is used to make cycle helmets to protect our heads.

Plastic shell

Foam lining

 How does insulating our homes save energy?

17

All wrapped up

Many of the things we buy are wrapped in plastic. The wrapping helps to keep things fresh. It can also tell us about the food we are buying. The words printed on a plastic yogurt pot tell us what flavor yogurt is inside.

◀ **If this bottle of water is dropped it will not break.**

Plastic is a good material for packaging because it doesn't break easily like glass. Plastic is very light compared with glass or metal. This means it is easier to transport plastic bottles to stores. Trucks need to use less fuel to transport plastic bottles.

▶ Plastic bottles keep chemicals safe.

Plastic is waterproof and can be resistant to chemicals. Plastic can be used to package harmful chemicals. Even if the plastic bottle is dropped the chemical won't spill because plastic is shatterproof.

The plastic wrapper keeps the food fresh.

Plastic packaging is safe and hygienic. It helps to keep food fresh for longer so that less food is wasted. It protects the food from being damaged. The plastic wrap we use to cover foods is strong, waterproof, airtight, and germproof.

 Can you name some things that come in plastic wrapping?

Plastic clothes

Some of our clothes are made from plastic. Fabrics made from plastic are easy to look after. They do not get dirty very easily or need much ironing. Plastic fabrics last a long time and do not lose their shape and become baggy.

◀ These threads are made from plastic.

Plastic fabrics are made by forcing hot, runny plastic through very fine holes in a machine. The plastic comes out in thin fibers that are used to weave into fabric. Fibers made from plastic are called **synthetic** fibers. Sometimes, synthetic fibers are mixed with natural ones such as cotton.

◀ **These clothes are made from plastic.**

A special type of plastic material is designed to be fireproof. This material is worn by firefighters and racing car drivers. Before it is used, the material is tested with a white-hot gas flame to make sure that it will protect whoever wears it.

Tents made from plastic cloth keep out the rain.

Fabric can be made waterproof by adding plastic. Some fabrics are just coated with plastic on one side. Other fabrics are put in a bath of plastic paste so that the paste soaks into the fabric.

 Are any of your clothes made from synthetic fabrics?

Plastics for health

Plastic can be used to keep us healthy. Hospitals use plastic because it is clean and safe. Plastic tubes are used in hospitals to give us medicine. Blood is stored in plastic bags. We are given injections with plastic syringes.

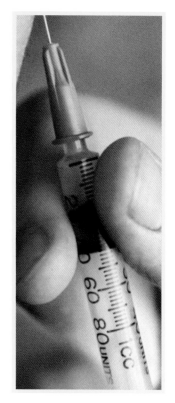

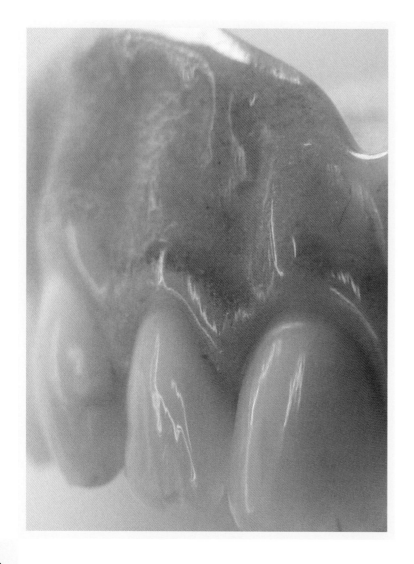

◀ **These teeth are made from plastic.**

As people grow older, they may lose their teeth. If this happens, they can have new ones made from plastic. Plastic teeth are hard and perfect for chewing. They are shaped to look exactly like our own teeth. Even better, they will never need fillings!

This plastic hand looks real.

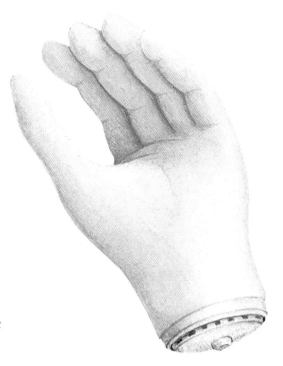

Plastic is used to make artificial parts of the body such as legs, arms, hands, and ears. They are made to look real and are used to replace those lost in accidents or through illness. Artificial legs help people to walk.

Plastic can help us move again.

When we get older, our joints, such as the hip or knee, sometimes wear away and become very painful. An artificial joint made from plastic and metal can be used to replace the damaged joint so that people can move again without pain.

 How do plastic caps on medicine bottles help keep children safe?

The problem with plastic

Plastic is a very useful material but it also causes problems. Plastic does not rot away. So if plastic bottles or bags are dropped on the ground then they stay there for a long time. Plastic litter spoils our environment.

◀ **A lot of plastic is thrown away.**

Every year we throw away millions of tons of plastic. Most of it ends up in **landfill sites** and is buried under the ground. Most plastics do not rot or break down so they will be there for a very long time.

◀ Plastic litter can hurt animals.

Plastic litter can damage wildlife. Many birds get tangled in plastic drinks can holders. The plastic holder gets wrapped around a bird's feet or neck. The bird may not be able to feed and may die. Animals that get trapped in plastic bags can suffocate.

Some plastic garbage is burned.

In some places, waste plastic is burned with other garbage in **incinerators**. When plastic is burned it gives off heat energy. This is used in some incinerators to produce electricity or hot water. The problem with burning plastic is that it releases poisonous gases into the air through the chimneys, and this causes **pollution**.

 How can you help to stop plastic harming the environment?

Recycling plastic

Plastic can be recycled and made into something new. This helps to save oil. Recycling plastic is difficult because there are so many different types of plastic. Each type of plastic is recycled in a different way.

◀ These plastic bottles have numbers printed on the bottom.

Different types of plastic need to be separated out before they can be recycled. Many plastic containers have a code number printed on them to show what type of plastic they are made from. This helps to sort the plastic out into different types ready for recycling.

These plastic bottles will be recycled.

Recycled plastic bottles are squashed into big blocks and taken to a factory. The plastic bottles are cut up into small flakes and washed and dried. Finally, they are melted down and made into new plastic objects.

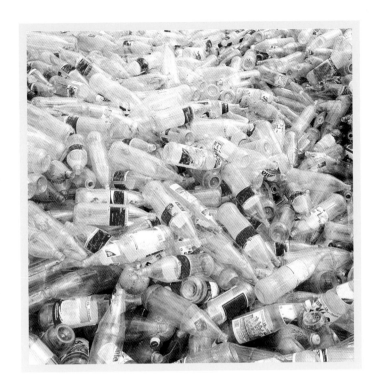

These things are made from recycled plastic.

Recycling our plastic helps to save oil. Nearly two tons of oil are saved every time a ton of polythene plastic is recycled. Recycled plastic is used to make many things such as furniture, seed trays, fences, sewer pipes, and carpets.

 What plastic things from school and home could you recycle?

Plastic for the future

The oil we use to make plastic is running out. Oil takes millions of years to form so we need to use other materials to make plastic. We can all help to save oil by using plastics carefully.

Wheat

Potatoes

Sugar

◀ **New plastics can be made from these foods.**

Scientists are developing new plastics that are made from food crops such as potatoes, sugar, wheat, oats, or even the shells of shellfish. In the future, our plastic will be made from these crops. These crops are renewable, which means they can be grown each year and will not run out like oil.

◀ **This flatware is made from plastic that will rot away.**

New plastics have been developed that will rot away when they are thrown out. **Biodegradable** plastics are used to make flatware which can be disposed of after it is used and made into compost.

Try to reuse plastic at school and home.

Plastic containers can be used for storing all sorts of things. Empty yogurt pots make great plant pots. Why not carry your shopping in a knapsack or basket instead of a plastic bag? Make sure you recycle any plastic you cannot reuse.

 Can you think of other ways to re-use plastic containers?

See how much you know!

What is most plastic made from?

How are plastic gloves made?

Why is plastic used to make electric sockets and cover wires?

Why are plastic bottles used for storing some chemicals?

What happens to plastic things that are thrown away?

How can you tell what type of plastic a container is made from?

What will plastic be made from in the future?

What plastic items could you reuse?

Key words

Bottle

Fabric	**Factory**
Foam	**Material**
Oil rig	**Recycling**
Tube	**Wrapping**

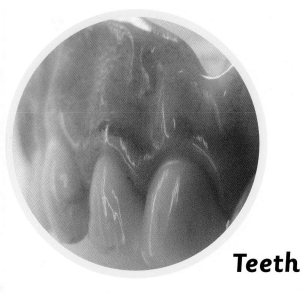

Teeth

Glossary

Biodegradable—When a material can be decayed by bacteria and other tiny animals.

Durable—When something is hard-wearing and lasts for a long time.

Flexible—Something that can easily bend.

Incinerator—A fire where unwanted things are burned and turned to ashes.

Insulator—A material or substance that heat does not easily pass through.

Landfill site—A huge hole in the ground where garbage is burned.

Pollution—Harmful chemicals, gases, or garbage that damage the environment.

Resistant—When a material is unharmed by things such as chemicals or heat.

Synthetic—Fabric made from plastic fibers.

Index

A
acrylic 13
artificial limbs 23

B
biodegradable 29, 31
bottles 12, 14, 18, 24, 26, 27, 30, 31

C
cellulose 8
chemicals 11, 19, 30, 31
clothing 8, 12, 13, 20-21
coal tar 9
cotton 8, 20

D
durable 9, 31

E
electricity 7, 25, 30
environment 10, 11, 24, 25, 31
extrusion 15

F
fabric 20, 21, 31

factory 10, 27, 31
fire 17, 21, 31
flexible 9, 12, 31
foam 13, 16, 17, 31
food 16, 18, 19, 28
fossil fuel 6

G
gloves 15, 30

H
health 22-23
heat 11, 12, 15, 16, 25, 31

I
incinerators 25, 31
insulation 16, 17, 31

L
landfill sites 24, 31

M
mold 9, 14, 15

O
oil 6, 10-11, 26, 27, 28

oil rig 10, 31

P
pollution 25, 31
polycarbonate 13
polystyrene 13, 17
polythene 11, 27
PVC 13

R
recycling 26-27, 29, 30, 31
refinery 10, 11
resistance 13, 19, 31

S
synthetic 20, 21, 31

T
teeth 22, 31
transparent 13
tube 14, 15, 22, 31

W
waterproof 7, 19, 21
wildlife 25
wrapping 18-19, 31

Photocredits:
Abbreviations: l-left, r-right, b-bottom, t-top, c-center, m-middle
Front cover — Photodisc. Back cover — Corbis. 4bl, 16bl, 28tl — BASF. 27cl, 27bl — BPI Recycled Products. 7br — Brand X Pictures. 6bl, 7tr, 10tr, 24t — Comstock. 4tl, 6tr, 7bl, 10bl, 13tr, 16tl, 20b, 22t, 23b — Corbis. 8b — John Deer Farming. 1, 3bl, 7tl, 12tl, 12ml, 21b, 24b, 26tr, 27tr — Digital Vision. 20t — EyeWire (Photodisc). 3tl, 5tl, 11bl, 14tr, 30t — Flat Earth. 5tr, 18bl, 31t — Image 100. 12bl, 13c, 13br, 17tl, 17br — Ingram Publishing. 5br, 22bl, 31b — Kingsbridge Dental Laboratory. 25t — Joe McDonald/Corbis. 8tl, 26tl, 26ml, 26bl, 29br — Simon Morse. 2-3, 31lmt, 5ml, 9br, 19tr, 21t, 25b, 30c — Photodisc. 14bl — Rexam. 13bl — Select Pictures. 5bl, 28lct, 28lcb, 28bl, 30b — Stockbyte. 9lm (inset) — The Telephone Museum. 9tr — Kien Vuong, UCSF-Drug Product Services Laboratory. 3lmb, 18tr, 19bl — USDA. 29tl — USDA Agricultural Research Service